STEAM AROUND READING

STEAM AROUND READING

KEVIN ROBERTSON

Despite fifteen years having elapsed since nationalization, the tender of No. 7816 *Frilsham Manor* still displays evidence of previous ownership at Reading, 2 December 1963. The engine is acting as the Up side pilot – there was a Down side pilot as well – with the tender well filled with what appears to be reasonable quality coal.

First published in 1998
This edition first published in 2009

Reprinted 2010

The History Press
The Mill, Brimscombe Port
Stroud, Gloucestershire, GL5 2QG
www.thehistorypress.co.uk

© Kevin Robertson, 1998, 2009

The right of Kevin Robertson to be identified as
the Author of this work has been asserted in accordance
with the Copyrights, Designs and Patents Act 1988.

British Library Cataloguing in Publication Data.
A catalogue record for this book is available from the British Library.

ISBN 978 0 7524 5330 9

Typesetting and origination by The History Press
Printed and bound in Great Britain by
Marston Book Services Limited, Oxford

CONTENTS

Introduction   7

1.   Reading, Great Western   9

2.   Reading Shed   31

3.   East towards Paddington   45

4.   The Southern Lines   63

5.   Towards Basingstoke & Westbury   73

6.   West to Bristol: Brunel's Billiard Table   81

7.   Interlude at Didcot   93

8.   Reading & Area: A Final Glimpse   99

According to its critics, the Great Western may well have had the motto 'if in doubt add a signal'. Certainly in the area of a large junction like Reading this may have appeared to be the case, but it probably contributed to the enviable safety record enjoyed by the company for many years. Like the steam engines though they are but a memory, this particular bracket being the Down relief inner homes for Reading East Main. The signal box of the same name is visible in the left background.

INTRODUCTION

In presenting the second in a personal series of railway photographs I am saddened in that the owner of the collection from which I have drawn heavily, Walter Gilburt, is no longer around to witness his views in print at last.

I had first met 'Wally', as he was known, some years previously and eventually it was agreed I could acquire his extensive collection of views and produce an album of these, as was indeed his wish. Small consolation perhaps then that this is the second – *Steam Around Eastleigh* was released in September 1997.

Wally's collection consists of well over a thousand negatives taken mainly in the early 1950s and centred on a number of his favourite locations. Reading was clearly one of these and as I too had spent much time using the station it seemed obvious that this should form the subject for the second in the series.

While in the process of collating the prints to be used it became apparent that there was also a small nucleus of prints available showing locations such as Southall and Didcot and so I have taken the liberty of including these as well. To broaden the scope a few of the views are not of Wally's taking but it is hoped that they will enhance the reader's interest.

It is frightening to recall that steam ceased through Reading over thirty years ago and even the number of diesel units that acted as those first replacements have themselves been consigned to memory. Perhaps there should be a sign, 'Nostalgia isn't what it used to be'.

Kevin Robertson

CHAPTER ONE

READING,
GREAT WESTERN

*Geographically Reading is for the most part situated on the gravel beds supporting the Rivers
Thames and Kennett, although it is to 'beer, seeds and biscuits' that the town owes its prosperity.
Sadly in the late twentieth century the local authority seems intent on disregarding such history
but sixty years ago such industry was regarded with pride, and excursions to Huntley & Palmer's
biscuit factory were a regular occurrence. One of these is seen at Reading General station on 5
August 1934. The engine is No. 4937 Lanelay Hall.*

Station approach, Christmas Day 1964. The main building dates from the 1840s although various additions and changes have been made over the years.

Probably the present-day Platform 4, complete with signs and vending machines of the period. The latter would appear to include Player's cigarettes and Fry's chocolate. Certain of the latter's machines were known to respond to a swift kick. Perhaps it was intentional that there is a 'penny in the slot' weighing machine next to the chocolates!

Midway along the platform were the Up main home signals for Reading East, depicted here on 22 April 1965. They, along with the rest of the mechanical signalling in the area, were superseded by colour lights shortly afterwards and indeed an interim phase is apparent in the form of the indicator attached to the bracket.

Reading, and an unidentified 'King' class 4–6–0 (only the first three digits of the number on the bufferbeam can be read with certainty, viz. 601) at what was then classified as the Down main platform. A date in the late 1940s is suggested by the generally drab scene and dingy coaching stock. On the left are the signals seen above, deliberately raised above the level of the platform canopy so as to be easier to read from a distance against the sky.

It appears that Wally's camera was of more interest to the gentleman on the Up platform than the approach of No. 5093 *Upton Castle*, 23 April 1950. In 1955 this platform was redesignated No. 5, replacing the somewhat complex numbering sequence dating from 1899.

On what could well be a test working, Brown Boveri gas turbine No. 18000 runs through the relief lines at Reading, heading for London, 3 June 1950. Although these were reasonably successful, pressure was subsequently exerted for the use of diesel locomotives as the successors to steam and No. 18000 was destined to have a working life of just ten years. Following some time in Europe both as a mobile test unit and later on a plinth, it was subsequently returned to the United Kingdom, although as a shell only and devoid of its turbine power plant.

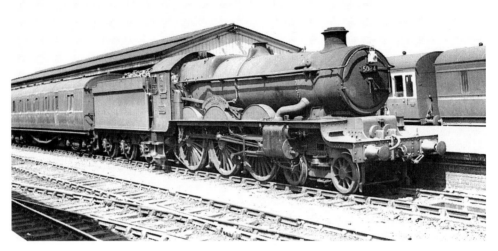

Formerly a member of the smaller 'Star' class, No. 5084 was rebuilt as a 'Castle' in 1937, although retaining its original name. It seems somewhat appropriate then to depict *Reading Abbey* within these pages, here at the head of what could well be a local working, 3 June 1950.

For comparison, *Reading Abbey* would originally have looked like this locomotive, No. 4053 *Princess Alexandra*, May 1953. The most obvious external differences are the boiler, the chimney size and cab. No. 4053 also sports the written insignia 'British Railways' on the tender and is attached to a collection of former Southern Railway 'Maunsell' corridor stock, thus indicating a through working.

Servicing a number of the faster stopping services were the large tank engines such as No. 6133. Generally popular with the crews, they possessed a good turn of speed and had a reasonable size cab. No. 6133 had been built in 1932 and remained in service until 1963. It is seen here on 3 June 1950.

Looking dated now perhaps, but almost 'art nouveau' when introduced in the 1930s. The GWR was among the first to recognize the potential for non-steam traction on certain services and a number of diesel railcars of similar type were introduced before the Second World War. Of these the first batch were designed as single units only – hence no buffers and drawing gear were provided. On what is probably a special working, No. W1 is seen leaving Reading eastbound on 27 May 1950.

An essential prerequisite in steam days was the provision of a pilot engine to add and detach vehicles from the various through services as well as provide a standby in the event of an engine failure. For this reason the shed foreman would usually allocate a somewhat run-down machine as otherwise crews would be tempted to exchange an engine for one perhaps better than their own. Reading would then be responsible for the repair or return working of the 'failure'. It could be that the pilot was itself awaiting a works visit for repair. Acting as pilot on 3 June 1950 was No. 4085 *Berkeley Castle*.

Another 'Castle', this time No. 5036 *Lyonshall Castle*, again on pilot work on the same day. It could well be that the engine is marshalling its own train judging from the Class 'A' headlights; unfortunately, Wally's notes do not record this detail.

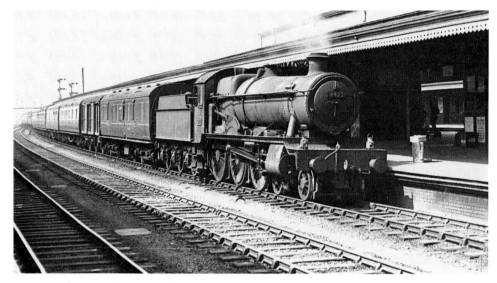

A particularly unusual formation behind No. 4923 *Evenley Hall* as it enters the Up main platform at Reading in April 1950. The train is of some considerable length while the engine is attached to one of the smaller 3,500 gallon tenders. Once again the working is not known, although it is probably in the 'express' category.

On 28 April 1965 a 'Western' diesel was derailed over the Caversham road bridge at the west end of the station, resulting in chaos all around. No. 6963 *Throwley Hall* was trapped in Platform 3, one of the dead end bays, and so restricted until matters could be resolved. Unfortunately no views of the derailment have been located. The crew of No. 6963 are also conspicuous by their absence.

How the mighty are fallen. The final days for No. 7011 *Banbury Castle* seemingly on freight work at Reading in 1963, although again with Class 'A' headlights. This was almost one of the last batch of 'Castle' class engines to appear in 1948, the design perpetuated at Swindon from 1923 through to 1950. No. 7011 had a short life of just seventeen years and was withdrawn in 1965.

Back to pilot working again and this time it is the turn of No. 6965 *Thirlestaine Hall* to be employed in removing two vehicles from the rear of a London-bound service, 23 April 1950. On the left is one of Reading's bay platforms, now Platform 7 and used for stopping services towards Didcot and Oxford.

For many years a Didcot-based engine – hence the '81E' code on the smokebox – No. 5935 *Norton Hall* stands in one of the middle roads at Reading, 3 June 1950. The fireman seems to have recently made the fire up judging from the smoke. No. 5935 was new from Swindon in 1932, one of twenty of the class built that year, and lasted in service until 1962.

One of the smaller 4–6–0s, No. 7819 *Hinton Manor*, on pilot work in late September 1962. Although the family resemblance in so far as design is apparent, the raised footplating allied to the smaller boiler made identification of the type easy from a distance.

Possibly a favourite among locomotive crews was the 'Grange' class, a basic go anywhere and do most things machine, at home on all but the very fastest and heaviest trains. This example is No. 6877 *Llanfair Grange*. For most if not all of its life this was a Worcester-based engine and is clearly then just a visitor to Reading, 3 June 1950. Notice also the 'GWR' insignia still visible on the tender.

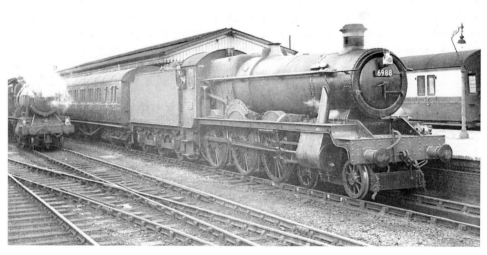

A modified 'Hall', No. 6988 *Swithland Hall*, on a stopping service, 27 May 1950. Compared with the original design, the '6959' class had a a number of modifications, including a plate frame at the front of the bogie, which is clearly visible here. Alongside is an unidentified member of the 43xx class.

Alongside what is now Platform 9, the Up relief line, No. 9305 has charge of a 'C' class working in the form of a parcels train, 3 June 1950. This can be determined from the position of the headlights – one at the base of the chimney and the other above the left-hand buffer. In this way signalmen and station staff could identify the type of train from a distance.

One of the big 38xx freight engines on what may well be a running-in turn following repair, judging from its relatively clean condition, 23 April 1950. Attached to the tender is a somewhat interesting six-wheeled brake van while behind the engine is an example of what was known as 'concertina' stock, so called because the doors had to be inset slightly from the bodywork to comply with the loading gauge.

An early 4–6–0, No. 4053 *Princess Alexandra*, eking out the last years of life on a through train from the Southern, 27 May 1950. (It is likely this is the same train seen with No. 31793 at its head on page 26.) Through the grime it is possible to make out the 'British Railways' wording on the tender, which was in the same style as the earlier 'Great Western' wording.

Waiting to depart for Paddington on 3 June 1950 is No. 5092 *Tresco Abbey*, carrying the identification '258' in addition to the express head code. Reporting numbers, as they were called, were an additional means of identifying a train's origin, although they were more usually carried in the form of metal digits attached to a frame on the smokebox. Clearly there was no such frame available when No. 5092 left its point of origin and recourse has been made to a cheap alternative – chalk.

Amid a mountain of mail sacks, No. 6921 *Borwick Hall* arrives from Oxford with a van train, 11 March 1965. Although mail is still carried by train, the railways no longer have a monopoly of this traffic. For many years Reading had special post office rooms on the Down side, where a number of GPO staff were based.

London bound, No. 7015 *Carn Brea Castle* leaves Platform 9 with a short six-coach train, 27 May 1950. Wally clearly favoured this particular view of the station, complete with the rather magnificent signal to give the photograph depth.

Associated more with some of the smaller branch lines was 14xx class, represented here by No. 1407, leaving the station, complete with auto coach in tow, bound for Twyford and Henley, 27 May 1950. Reading had two of these small but well-proportioned engines for some time (No. 1444 was the other) and they were used on certain local branch services as well as occasional main line stopping services outside peak hours.

Displaying the first BR insignia on the tender and probably also in lined black livery, No. 4931 *Hanbury Hall* departs light engine, 27 May 1950.

A final view from this location shows No. 6113 in charge of a typical stopping service for Slough and Paddington, May 1950. In the background the tracks lead to and from the relief line platforms, while beyond these are the two through goods roads and then the descent to the signal works.

Busy times at the west end of the station, with No. 7816 *Frilsham Manor* nearest the camera at the head of the 1.20 p.m. Basingstoke vans, 11 March 1965. Entering in the opposite direction is No. 6841 *Marlais Grange*, while an unidentified 'Western' class diesel-hydraulic is also departing. The signals are in the intermediate stage of changeover with both semaphore and colour light equipment on the gantry.

Special working of the now preserved No. 7808 *Cookham Manor* at the head of the Locomotive Club of Great Britain 'North and West Limited Rail Tour', 21 June 1964. The engine is displaying the white-painted hinges to the smokebox door, which style adorned a number of machines in the final months of steam working. Interestingly the station announcer had advised waiting passengers that this was the special train to Craven Arms.

Another special working, with No. 5054 *Earl of Ducie* in charge of an OURS (Oxford University Railway Society) train from Paddington to Worcester, 16 May 1964. No. 5054 was regarded as one of the best of the 'Castles' left in service and yet, despite its seemingly excellent external condition with no steam leaks, it was withdrawn and cut up for scrap within a few months.

Probably the same working depicted earlier with No. 4053 in charge (see page 21), although this time former Southern Mogul No. 31793 has the train. This is probably a through working to the former Southern lines, possibly even a Birkenhead to Brighton train.

The final months of steam working. No. 7029 *Clun Castle* is at the head of the 9.45 (SO) Paddington to Weston-Super-Mare, 20 July 1963. Two years later this same engine would have the melancholy distinction of hauling the last regular steam-drawn service out of Paddington. The last of a class of 171 engines to remain in service, it is now preserved at Birmingham Tyseley.

An unusual and seldom photographed vehicle, a bullion van of which five were built in batches between 1903 and 1913. Originally intended for the carriage of gold from the ocean liners at Plymouth to London, for security they were provided with doors on one side only and so care was needed to ensure the train in which they were marshalled arrived at a platform on the correct side. What is believed to be W819W was recorded at Reading on 21 May 1965, although it is not noted to what use it was then being put.

Transition from steam – a grimy and nameless 'Hall' No. 6917, formerly *Oldlands Hall*, shunting at Reading during the early morning of 29 April 1965. Alongside is a 'Western' class diesel which has taken over from steam with a Paddington express working.

A rarity in the form of one of the short-lived Bristol Pullman trains alongside the prototype Mark 2 'XP64' stock at Reading, 20 April 1965. The eight-coach Pullman units were similar to sets operating on the Midland Region at this time, although they suffered the same complaints of harsh riding. In many respects they were the forerunners of today's HST services, although the latter are available to all passengers and not just a select few.

A through goods working with another Southern engine, No. 31796, running along the goods relief lines, 23 April 1950. Aside from passengers there was considerable transfer of goods at the station, which continues to be the case even today.

The bays now at the west end of the station, looking towards the buffer stops. On the extreme right stopping services would usually commence for Newbury, while the centre platform was used for Basingstoke locals. The platform at which the rear end of the train is visible was mainly for parcels and pilot use, similar arrangements applying to this day.

Seen from the opposite direction, Platform 1 for Newbury has a lengthy train stabled alongside. Between Nos 2 and 3 the connecting trusses were later replaced by sections of plain girder.

Entering Platform 3 is No. 6826 *Nannerth Grange* with the 3.35 p.m. Trowbridge to Reading stopping service, 12 July 1963.

On a cold January day in 1964 No. 6107 awaits departure with the 1.30 p.m. vans for Basingstoke. Alongside is one of the first generation DMUs, at that time still required to display an old-fashioned oil tail-lamp at the rear.

CHAPTER TWO

READING SHED

Reading steam shed was situated beyond the station and at a slightly lower level than the main line. The turntable was at the rear of the shed and is seen here with former Great Central design R.O.D. No. 3038 being manually moved, 23 April 1950. These engines were not popular on the Western compared with the home-grown heavy freight design and it would be interesting to know the thoughts of the crew at this stage.

The front of the shed this time, with the repair shop on the right. No. 5002 *Ludlow Castle*, having been serviced, awaits its next turn of duty. There would not be many more, however, for the engine was withdrawn in the same year the photograph was taken, 1964.

Outside-framed goods No. 2369 on shed. These engines dated back to the nineteenth century and were at one time part of the standard goods type. Increasing train weights, however, allied to newer and larger machines, rendered them redundant and No. 2369 was withdrawn before 1940.

A trio of 61xx tank engines – Reading had no fewer than nine of the type in 1947 – outside the shed, 19 July 1959. For the record two can be identified, Nos 6117 and 6150, which, judging from the filled bunkers, are ready to leave, probably for London-bound workings.

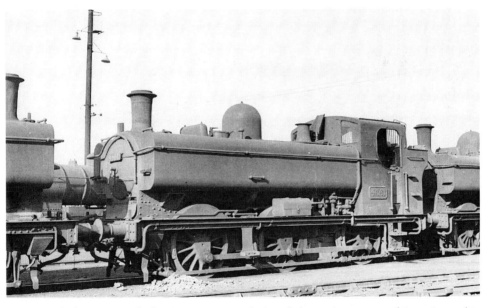

For general shunting work the Great Western designed the various types of 'pannier tank', so called because of the obvious position of the water tanks. The advantage was that it was possible to gain easier access to the inside motion for oiling compared with the side tank design preferred by other companies. Resting between duties at Reading on 23 April 1950 is No. 4661 with two unidentified sister engines.

Churchward design 'Mogul' No. 6302 on shed, April 1950. The ground-level shot allows a good view of the Automatic Train Control shoe under the buffer beam, which was a feature of safe working on the Great Western for a number of decades.

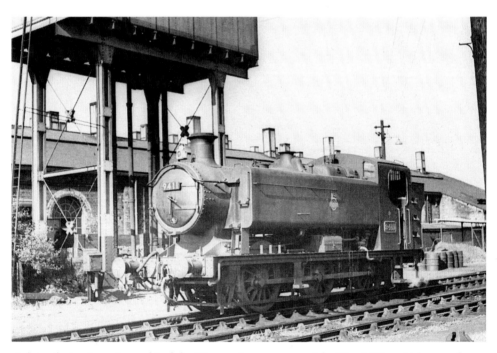

A later design 'pannier tank' of the 94xx series, represented by No. 9411, which was almost brand new in 1950.

From the latest to the oldest, or older to be more exact, 'Bulldog' No. 3454 *Skylark* in the twilight of its active life at Reading, April 1950. Again the connection with earlier years is apparent in the form of the outside frames, while the tender would again appear to be embellished with the letters 'GWR'.

Often to be found on various freight workings, the 63xx class could be regarded as difficult for the fireman unless the ash pan draughting was exact. When set correctly and in reasonable condition, however, they would perform prodigious feats and consequently it was very much a question of 'love them or hate them'.

Another pannier, No. 9791, at Reading, June 1950. Two or three of these engines would be at work almost continuously in the various yards, twenty-four hours a day, the residents seemingly accepting the continual crashing of wagon buffers as the norm.

Skylark again and this time in steam, June 1950. No doubt to a harassed shed foreman any engine that could turn a wheel was useful, although usage for No. 3454 was probably restricted to local freight workings.

Riddles design 2–8–0, then No. 70876, April 1950. Several hundred of the type were built in the 1940s to assist in covering locomotive shortages and a number were also sent for work in Europe. Not always popular with the crews, they were basic and functional machines, the majority later finding employment in the north of the country where a number lasted almost to the very end of steam working.

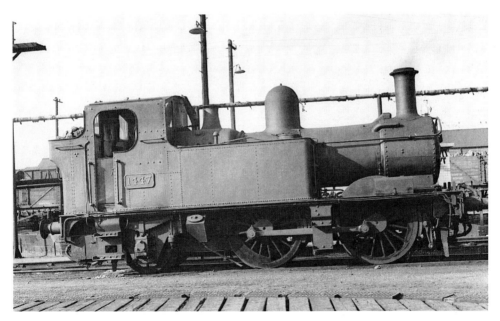

Another 14xx, No. 1447, parallel to the shed turntable, April 1950. For small engines they possessed a remarkable turn of speed and it is said almost 70 m.p.h. was reached on one occasion. As a result of the short wheelbase, what the conditions were like for the crew at such speed is best left to the imagination.

A former Southern design, No. 30783 *Sir Gillemere*, being turned on the turntable, June 1950. The presence of an engine of this type is explained by the numerous through workings, as a result of which engine changing would often occur at Reading. This was a feature of the steam age and would continue almost to the very end of steam working.

Looking somewhat travel weary is No. 6996 *Blackwell Hall*, possibly sporting all over black livery. Wally has also recorded much of the general clutter of the shed, the coal wagon in the background, oil drums and, of course, ash and clinker. Matters would get progressively worse as the years passed and labour became more and more difficult to obtain. It is perhaps fortunate for the railways that health and safety at work legislation was then in its infancy.

Another relic from a previous generation was saddle tank No. 1925, which for many years had found regular employment on the branch from Newbury to Lambourn. With this run now considered too strenuous its final days were spent either shunting the shed or at the nearby signal works, although the open cab would have made bunker-first working somewhat unpleasant at times. Steam was also not a popular choice within the works themselves as the buildings would fill with smoke and there was only limited ventilation.

The story of *City of Truro* has been recounted many times elsewhere, although views of the engine at Reading are perhaps less well known. Here she is seen complete with 'RCTS' headboard on 28 April 1957 and in her usual pristine condition. The similarity to *Skylark* is readily apparent, although in the case of No. 3440 the driving wheels will be seen to be of larger diameter.

The final sequence of views of the shed depict the location and shed occupants during the last months of steam working, commencing with an interior view of No. 7900, formerly *St Peter's Hall*, now bereft of nameplates on the very day of closure, 3 January 1965. By this time only three steam engines were present, Nos 7900, 6106 and 6984. Although No. 7900 had been officially withdrawn, there does seem to be smoke emanating from the chimney.

Towards the end of steam working cleaning was either limited or non-existent, as shown by the grime adhering to the sides of No. 4661. Maintenance too was limited, men either having left for better-paid jobs in other areas or being seconded to retrain and work on the newer diesels.

No. 7816 *Frilsham Manor* again, still with 'GWR' on the tender. From the look of the white stain running down from the safety valves and top feed, the engine has been priming at some stage, indicating she was running when somewhat overdue for a boiler washout.

61xx tanks, Nos 6161 and 6125, seen from either end. The photograph was taken in September 1964 with even the shed looking somewhat worse for wear with missing glass panels. Note the indentation on the top of the bunker of No. 6161, which was necessary should the headcode dictate a lamp be placed on the top bracket.

London Midland design Ivatt 2–6–0 No. 43007 at Reading in December 1964. A modern if somewhat ugly machine, it was complete with high running plate and consequently exposed pipework and fittings, which nevertheless made for ease of maintenance. No. 43007 has definitely been priming at some time – note the numerous white streaks down the smokebox.

Peering into the gloom, No. 6874 *Haughton Grange* is head to head with Southern 4–6–2 No. 34084 *253 Squadron*, the latter reported as being under repair. It was somewhat unusual for a Southern engine to be repaired in this way; normally maintenance would be carried out when the engine arrived back at its home depot or worked back light engine. Clearly though this was not possible in this case and Waterloo would no doubt be invoiced accordingly for the time and costs involved.

Fitted for snow plough duty, No. 2261 is standing outside the shed, 24 February 1963. It was common practice for an engine to be so equipped semi-permanently during the winter season, one advantage of steam traction being that a steam lance was also available to clear frozen points if this was necessary.

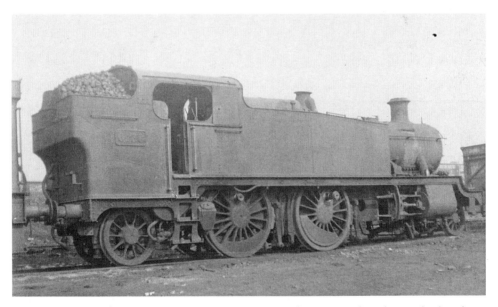

Temporarily reposing as a 2–2–2T, No. 6130 awaits the return of its front wheelset from repair, 24 February 1963. Work such as this would be possible within the shed lifting shop, although care would be required in moving No. 6130 to avoid placing undue strain on the remaining bearings.

Devoid of engines Reading shed awaits its fate, January 1963. Occasional steam workings still passed the station at this time, although if servicing were required Didcot and Southall were the nearest points of assistance. The shed site was later rebuilt as a diesel depot and is still in use today.

Replacing steam as a shunter at the signal works was this 1956-built Ruston & Hornsby chain-driven diesel mechanical locomotive, which supplemented an existing small diesel already on site. Carrying the identification of No. 20, when not in use it often reposed in this position, where it was photographed on 23 January 1965. Some years later the identification was changed to 97020 and it survived in service until April 1981.

CHAPTER THREE

EAST TOWARDS PADDINGTON

No. 5901 Hazel Hall on an Up goods about to pass the main water tank and hydraulic house just east of the station, December 1963. Originally the hydraulic house supplied power for the lifts at the main station but the advent of electricity meant it was quickly rendered obsolete. The building was then put to a number of uses, one of which was as a workshop for the permanent way maintenance department.

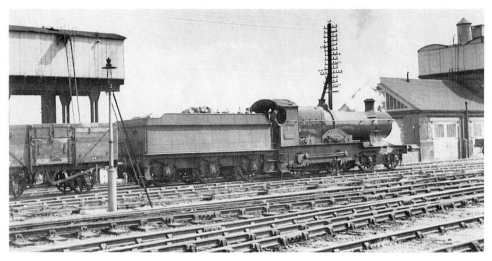

A final view of No. 3454 *Skylark*, clearly not in the best of condition judging from the escaping steam. Notice on the top of the cab the storm sheet, which would be attached to the front of the tender when required, so providing a certain degree of protection. The tall telegraph pole is yet another long gone item, although Wally has almost made it appear part of the engine itself! The train has left the west yard and no doubt represents a working towards Slough, possibly as far as London.

The *Rambling Rose* special of 23 March 1963, which took in a number of routes around Reading. The train was hauled by a Southern 'M7' 0–4–4T and is seen first arriving at the station from Basingstoke before reversing back into Platform 9. The hydraulic house is perhaps best remembered for the large advert for Huntley & Palmer's biscuits at the far end of the building.

A sad-looking No. 6854 *Roundhill Grange* in its last months of service at Reading West Yard, July 1965. With the loss of the smokebox number-plate someone has painted the engine number on – judging from the terrible external condition this is perhaps the only attention the engine has received for some time.

East now from Reading and upon passing the new connection between the Western and Southern lines a good view of the former Southern steam shed could be obtained. Coming up the steep climb from the Southern is a D65xx diesel, which will no doubt have its work cut out after being checked at signals on the bank itself.

On a bleak January day, D864 heads towards Paddington in charge of a rake of BR Mark 1 stock. In the foreground are various sidings formerly on the approach to Reading Southern station while the photograph was taken from near the gasworks, itself also rail connected for many years.

Beyond Reading towards Twyford the railway passed through Sonning cutting, the location of countless railway photographs over the years. By way of a change I have included just one and not even of a typical Western product, depicting instead SR 'Merchant Navy' No. 35005 *Canadian Pacific* at the head of a railtour, May 1965.

To Twyford now and No. 5062 *Earl of Shaftesbury* is passing the rear of Twyford West signal box, eastbound for Paddington, 10 April 1954. The engine has thirteen coaches in tow and yet seems to be running well, although no doubt the fireman will be glad to reach Paddington. In the background the goods shed can just be glimpsed while nearer to the signal-box is a very small store hut complete with chimney and stove.

On less exacting duties and on the same date, No. 5932 *Haydon Hall* awaits departure with an Up parcels working. The coaching stock is definitely varied and includes two SR utility vans towards the rear of the train. As can be seen from the running in board, Twyford was the junction for Henley, the branch to this location curving away behind the train as well as having its own bay platform.

No. 6123 this time on a London-bound stopper, typical of the work performed by members of the class from Reading. The station is largely unaltered today and still retains the wide gap between the platforms, a legacy of the earliest days of the broad gauge.

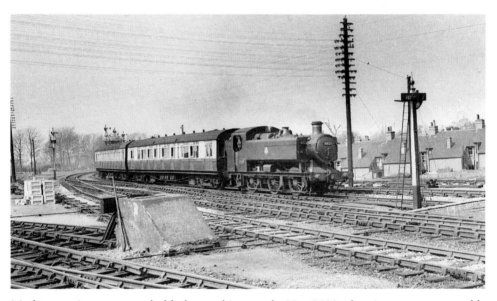

Modern motive power and elderly coaching stock: No. 9403, then just seven years old, at the head of two former concertina slip coaches forming the Henley branch service, 10 April 1954. The combination is just entering the bay platform at Twyford from Henley, with the connections to the rest of the system visible in the foreground. The wooden post starting signal from the bay platform is also an absolute delight, the old-style wording that accompanied such signals still in place years after the practice was superseded.

During the morning and evening peaks through trains operated between Henley and Paddington, one of which is seen here first at Twyford and then at the intermediate branch station of Shiplake with No. 5038 *Morlais Castle* in charge, 30 May 1963. Somehow it seemed strange having a 'Castle' at the head of what was in effect a branch passenger train, yet the service continued for many years and even today there are through diesel trains during peak times.

No. 5038 at rest outside the overall roof at Henley, having arrived on the 5.20 p.m. from Paddington. At this time the branch was double track throughout, with numerous sidings and even a turntable at the terminus. It also saw considerable seasonal traffic associated with the annual regatta. All this has changed over the years though and the route now operates as a single line from Twyford.

Returning to the main line, which was four track all the way between Reading and Paddington, and to another special working, 25 April 1954. This time it is the turn of 'Dukedog' 4–4–0s, Nos 9023 and 9011, making a good turn of speed on an 'RCTS' train. Not normally seen in the London area, the class was almost exclusively based on the former Cambrian section but was slowly displaced by more modern motive power from the early 1950s onwards.

Despite having locomotives that mostly bore a family resemblance to one another, the same could certainly not be said for the trains they pulled, few services aside from the prestige workings having rolling stock of like design in their formation. A good example is this passenger working near Twyford on 25 April 1954, with No. 6935 *Browsholme Hall* in charge. The train is a mixture of Churchward and Collett stock and probably mixed liveries as well.

Further east still and we come to the reception yard at Southall. No. 6983 *Otterington Hall* has just arrived from Reading, 28 April 1965. As late as the 1970s trip workings such as these were commonplace although they have now given way to bulk train movements only, with the consequent closure of numerous wayside yards.

Southall shed seen from the window of a passing train, May 1965. Southall was the last steam shed on the former Western lines in the London area and later took on a new role as a maintenance depot for diesel multiple units. Even at this late stage in its career there are a number of steam engines visible as well as the 'Warship' diesel nearest the camera. The depot remained in use until the 1980s and has since become a home for steam engines employed on special workings from London.

A visit to the shed the previous year revealed locomotives of both BR and GWR design as well as a DMU. In steam are Nos 92243 and 6961 *Stedham Hall*, as well as a 61xx – possibly No. 6165. Unfortunately the general area also shows signs of lack of care, judging from the piles of ash and clinker.

A sad sight at the shed in 1964 were rows of locomotives condemned and awaiting their call to the scrapyard. Leading the lineup is No. 2841, and behind is No. 5070, formerly *Sir Daniel Gooch*, the 28xx having been withdrawn the previous year.

Three former Austerity 2–8–0s were also to be seen – Nos 90174, 90630 and 90693 – and it is unlikely any of these were required for service again.

One of the big and superbly proportioned 47xx class, No. 4705, at Southall on a very wet Sunday, 17 March 1963. The engine is clearly devoid of its front pony truck, although whether this was repaired and put back into traffic or had arrived for temporary fixing before scrapping is not recorded.

Away from the shed there was also interesting movement at the Southall gasworks located just west of the station and north of the running lines. In this view both steam and diesel motive power are visible, although as was often the case when viewed from a train they were stationary.

Having ventured east from Reading it would be inappropriate not to travel the final few miles to Old Oak Common, home of the London steam depot of the GWR. This was also the largest shed both physically and in terms of allocation of engines, and as it was the starting point for a number of fast workings it also had the most express engines on its books. One is seen here, No. 6021 *King Richard II*, in a line of others of its type, 29 August 1954.

Despite an often acute shortage of cleaners in the later years, those who were available were normally set to work on passenger engines. No. 4078 *Pembroke Castle* displays the results of an amount of elbow grease as it reposes at Old Oak in August 1964.

Doyen of the class, No. 6000 *King George V*, readily identifiable by the bell carried on the front framing. Seen from this angle the two most obvious differences between this and the slightly smaller 'Castle' class are apparent, namely the larger boiler and outside bearings on the front bogie axle.

Last in the line of Great Western 4–6–0s were the 'County' class. The family likeness did not necessarily mean it was regarded in the same light by certain of the footplate crews. Perhaps this is one of the reasons why No. 1005 *County of Devon* looks somewhat tired in comparison with the other views Wally took at Old Oak on the same day. No. 1005 was built in 1945 and withdrawn after just eighteen years service in the early 1960s.

Attached to a later flat-sided tender, No. 7025 *Sudeley Castle* could do with a wipe over with an oily rag, at Old Oak, August 1964.

Another 'King', this time No. 6012 *King Edward VI*, displaying the early type of BR insignia, cruelly known as the cycling lion, on the tender.

The Western Region were also allocated a number of BR Standard 'Pacifics', which were best received at Cardiff. Elsewhere it was a question of a machine that was vastly different, which is exemplified in the high running plate and outside valve gear. Eventually the batch was re-allocated away from the Western, but not before No. 70026 *Polar Star* had been recorded on shed, August 1954.

A final view of No. 6012, included to show the apparent burn mark at the bottom of the smokebox door. This was probably due to a buildup of hot cinders against the door itself caused by the engine being worked hard over a considerable distance.

For shunting around the area there were of course the ubiquitous pannier tanks, although the final design of these also differed from the originals in having outside cylinders and a short wheelbase. Accordingly they would pitch and roll on poor track at any speed and were best described as somewhat lively. Nevertheless they were powerful machines and when coupled to a heavy rake of coaches could move these in and out of the terminus at Paddington with commensurate ease. No. 1503 is here seen on less exacting tasks, August 1964.

A final view of a 'King' at the depot. No. 6024 *King Edward I* was modified with a mechanical lubricator, the box for which is visible just behind the outside steam pipe.

Returning to Reading now and to Huntley & Palmer's factory, which had its own motive power for shunting the extensive siding facilities. This is their No. 1, a fireless steam locomotive dating from 1932, which survived to pass into preservation in 1970. At least six engines are known to have worked at the site between 1875 and 1969, when rail access ceased. The company produced a number of well-known biscuit brands, including at one time a 'Great Western Selection', served in the dining cars of the company before 1939.

On the subject of industrial locomotives, this is a 150 h.p. Fowler diesel from Reading gasworks, recorded in the early 1960s before production ceased on the site in 1965.

CHAPTER FOUR
THE SOUTHERN LINES

The Southern station at Reading with a 'Mogul' awaiting departure, 1965. The town itself is in the background, complete with tower crane, while in the immediate foreground is the coal yard belonging to Messrs Toomers.

No. 31799 at the electrified platform at Reading Southern in charge of the 11.05 a.m. Redhill train, 25 April 1964. Steam and electric worked hand in hand from the station almost to the very end, while even now, thirty years later, not all the routes served by the former Southern from Reading have been electrified and there are a number of diesel workings towards Redhill and the like.

No. 31870 at the station, which has arrived on the 1.35 p.m. from Redhill, July 1963. Beneath the canopy it is just possible to glimpse a number of trolleys and barrows, even the design of these having changed over the years.

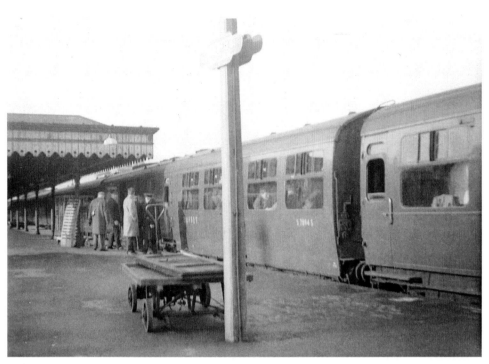

A buffet car at Reading South was a rarity, but it is explained in that this was a special working in connection with a 'Locomotive Club of Great Britain' rail tour, 3 January 1965.

Reading Southern shed, a three-road affair open at either end and easily visible from the Western main line, 7 April 1965. In the background too is the Southern signal-box, while reposing outside the shed in the morning sunshine is No. 31791.

Some few years earlier, in May 1950, Wally recorded former South Eastern 4–4–0 No. 1217 outside the shed but with the gaunt background of the Great Western East signal-box also visible. These 4–4–0s had held sway with many of the workings from Reading for many years but were gradually superseded by the 'Mogul' type.

A line of Southern types, left to right Nos 31857, 31615 and 33004, possibly all in steam, Christmas Day 1962. The Southern was no better at cleaning engines than the Western, some might say worse, while conditions for working on the engines were limited both here and at most other Southern sheds.

Two years later and this time at the height of summer, only two locomotives are to be seen, Nos 33027 and 31400. The shed area looks just as cluttered as previously. Indeed it is unlikely much was done afterwards, although walking around at night amid piles of ash and clinker discarded by various engines could be fraught with danger.

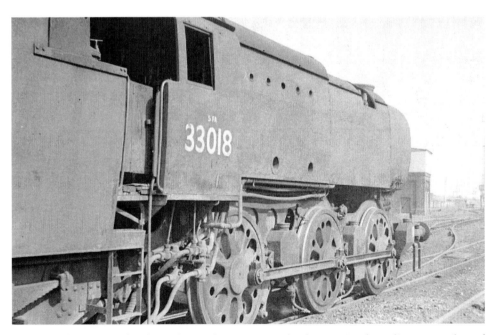

To work the various freight and parcels turns over the former Southern lines a number of 'Q1' class 0–6–0s were based at the depot. No. 33018 was efficient and functional even if alien in appearance. The class was introduced at a time of need in 1942 and did sterling service for many years until withdrawn in 1966.

Alongside a very dilapidated shed, No. 31791 reposes amid clouds of escaping steam, 28 December 1965. Officially the shed had been closed in January 1965, although it continued to be used by steam engines for a period afterwards.

At the east end of the site was a 65 ft turntable, with No. 31408 making use of the facility in April 1965. For its final years the depot was a sub-shed of Guildford. The Guildford shed itself retained steam operation until the very end in July 1967.

The funeral train for Sir Winston Churchill leaving the Southern lines at Reading, making its way towards the Western and its eventual destination near Oxford, January 1965. The engine is appropriately No. 34051 *Sir Winston Churchill*, the sad cortège having left Waterloo and then run via Clapham Junction and Richmond in order to reach Reading. As a result of the attendant publicity surrounding the working, No. 34051 was secured for official preservation but has been only a static exhibit at various sites for several years now.

Reading gasworks, Sunday 3 March 1963. BR Standard 4–6–0 No. 73085 *Melisande* is shunting the Nine Elms breakdown train before a gas condenser was unloaded at the gasworks. The actual condenser had arrived by road from Aldershot and was taken to the nearby Reading Southern station (Reading South) for loading on to a rail wagon and the subsequent short journey to the actual gasworks. The views show the preparation of the site and hoisting of the condenser into place. (G.R. May)

Along the Southern main line now to Earley and a light engine working, No. 30837, returning to its home depot at Feltham, 4 May 1965.

Wokingham level crossing, which caused considerable traffic congestion even in 1963. The train is signalled to take the former SECR route towards Farnborough and Ash. The eventual destination was probably Guildford.

CHAPTER FIVE

TOWARDS BASINGSTOKE
& WESTBURY

Returning to the Western lines now and at Reading West Curve the unusual sight of a tender-first working. The engine is No. 34103 Calstock *and the occasion a failed diesel unit, resulting in the steam engine being purloined at short notice to work through to Basingstoke on a stopping service, 6 February 1965.*

Reading West station and No. 6803 *Buklebury Grange* is at the head of a Basingstoke to Birmingham freight, probably early 1965. Ahead of the engine the line curves away towards the Western main line and Didcot while Reading General station could be accessed by taking the route to the right. The sidings in the centre were by then part of the DMU service facility.

Approaching Reading West from Reading General direction is No. 6989 *Wightwick Hall* at the head of the 5.05 p.m. Paddington to Hungerford working. To the left is Oxford Road Junction signal-box and while the Up platform is in its original timber form, that on the Down side has been replaced by concrete.

Another wet day and this time it is the turn of No. 34037 *Clovelly* to be in charge of a York–Bournemouth through working, which it has probably taken over at Oxford. Through trains still run from the South Coast to the Midlands and North but instead now use the main station at Reading, thus involving a reversal in direction.

Just to prove it did not always rain at Reading, No. 6131 enjoying fine weather on the 7.02 a.m. Reading to Southampton service, 27 June 1964. It would take this train as far as Basingstoke.

Running light is No. 44833, which was returning towards Didcot and its Midlands home from the Southern Region, 2 May 1965.

From the high vantage point of Tilehurst Road bridge a green liveried DMU heads a Reading to Newbury stopping service, 6 April 1965. Notice on the opposite line the ATC ramp, which was always placed slightly angled to the rails themselves to avoid creating a furrow in the contact show of locomotives.

Tilehurst Road bridge itself, seen from the opposite side. No. 73029 is in charge of the 11.00 a.m. Bournemouth West to York train, early April 1965.

Round to Southcote junction now and the point of divergence for the goods line to Coley, seen curving away to the right, and also the routes to Basingstoke and Hungerford. No. 6963 *Throwley Hall* is in charge of an unknown 'LCGB' working on 2 May 1965. The engine was withdrawn shortly afterwards.

The original Brunel chalet design at Mortimer, witness to No. 34040 *Crewkerne* passing in charge of the northbound 'Pines Express', May 1965. After 1962 this service was routed away from the Somerset and Dorset and instead took in the line through Southampton and Reading to Oxford and the Midlands, lasting until July 1967.

Returning to the other section of the original Berks and Hants and this time towards Hungerford, where at Theale No. 4991 *Cobham Hall* is passing with the evening Paddington to Hungerford working, May 1963. Theale still survives today and handles much in the way of railborne stone and petroleum traffic, although a consequence of this has been a necessary remodelling of the station environment and the loss of the original station buildings, part of which can be seen on the left-hand side.

To Aldermaston now and the turn of No. *6955 Lydcott Hall* to be at the head of the 3.15 p.m. Westbury to Reading working, April 1963. Today the station has little more than bus shelter-type buildings on each platform, although as can be seen masonry structures were originally provided.

The sunshine catches No. *6994 Baggrave Hall* waiting at the Up platform at Newbury with what may well be a train from Weymouth, 8 August 1956. Behind the engine is a rake of relatively new Mk 1 stock, indicating the importance of the working compared with a stopping service.

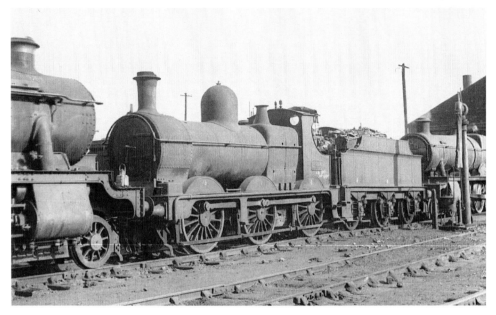

Our final destination on the Berks and Hants line is the shed at Westbury, where in October 1950 Wally recorded Dean Goods No. 2444 on shed. At this time there were still fifty of the Victorian design theoretically 'on the books', although many would be withdrawn without achieving much further work. No. 2444 lasted until 1952 while the last of the class was withdrawn in 1957. One, No. 2516, is preserved in Swindon Railway Museum.

Wally then turned his attention to the engine in front of the Dean, No. 6982 *Melmerby Hall*. Westbury had an allocation of some twenty 4–6–0 types, which were used on a variety of duties, including workings to Bristol, Reading and the West Country.

CHAPTER SIX

WEST TO BRISTOL:
BRUNEL'S BILLIARD TABLE

Returning to the Reading area now, but heading west along the main line towards Didcot. Scours Lane Junction was between Reading and Tilehurst and the site of a number of crossovers between the various running lines as well as the western end of Reading West yard. Running in from the direction of Didcot, with steam seemingly leaking from every gland, is No. 73112, its train consisting of a mixture of tank cars and open wagons, 20 April 1965.

Permanent way work east of Reading and a view of a ballast train with No. 3855 in charge, 27 February 1965. This picture gives a good view of the local permanent way gang hut complete with grindstone.

Tilehurst station served the western suburbs of Reading. There was also a small goods yard on the Down line at the east end of the station, which No. 8720 is passing on another engineer's train, July 1963.

Notices at Tilehurst in June 1965, that to the right announcing the closure of Reading South and the transfer of its passenger services to Reading General.

The four-track section of main line continued beyond Tilehurst, and on a snowy March day in 1965 No. 3848 is rushing through with empty wagons. The 38xx class benefited slightly by having a larger cab compared with the older 28xx series, although even so conditions would have been testing on the footplate.

For some time during the early years of the century Tilehurst even boasted a slip coach service from Paddington, which would be shunted into a siding near the lamp hut on the right. Such facilities were long gone though when No. 34048 *Crediton* was recorded heading for Oxford with a through service from the Southern Region, 24 April 1965.

London Midland types were on occasions also seen in the Reading area, No. 48061 having arrived from Eastleigh and returning in its home direction. At the front at least the engine appears passably clean, although this is certainly not the case for the rest of the machine.

Bunker-first working now for No. 9450 as it heads for Reading, April 1963. Beyond the station on the far side of the Down line is the River Thames, the railway running almost parallel with the river from this point and accordingly meandering gently for some little distance.

Tender first now for No. 6924 *Grantley Hall*, relegated to permanent way duties in August 1964. The engine still retains its name-plate for the time being although several were later removed, either officially or otherwise. No. 6924 was withdrawn the following year.

Most of the express passenger workings on the Western had by now been handed over from steam to diesel, while changes were also taking place with the signalling around Reading. There are colour lights on both the Down main and Down relief but the Up lines retain semaphores for the time being. Brush Type 4, later Class 47, No. D1737 rushes through Tilehurst, March 1965. These engines, though efficient, were not necessarily popular in winter, the cabs being prone to draughts. Accordingly men would stuff newspaper into every crack in an attempt to make conditions bearable.

Despite steam being by then almost vanquished from the Western, the Southern retained front-line steam operation until July 1967, which meant a number of the through workings were still steam hauled. Here No. 34044 *Woolacombe* is on the Up main line at Tilehurst with the 'Pine's Express', June 1965.

Another LMR 8F and this time a rather tired-looking No. 48411 passing light through the station in the direction of Didcot, 12 June 1965. Its reason for being in the area is not reported.

Flying Scotsman at Tilehurst with a railway society special which had originated from Eastleigh, August 1964.

Because of the close proximity of the River Thames – the railway runs in a cutting just west of Tilehurst – the various overbridges afford a good vantage point for the photographer. From one of these No. *6965 Thirlestaine Hall* was recorded, heading towards Reading, on one of its final duties before withdrawal in 1965.

Purley this time, and No. 7819 *Hinton Manor* in charge of the Saturdays-only Hastings to Birmingham through working, 17 August 1963.

A cold February morning and No. 6962 *Soughton Hall* is working empty mineral wagons in the direction of Reading.

The legacy of the broad gauge is apparent in the width between the platforms at Goring, although this does appear to narrow somewhat in the distance. No. 5066 *Sir Felix Pole*, named after perhaps the most famous of all the GWR general managers, is running towards London on a named express in 1954.

Another view of the northbound 'Pine's Express' which sadly never seemed to carry its headboard in the final years, headed by No. 34050 *Royal Observer Corps* passing non-stop through Goring.

Sister engine to No. 4705 (see page 56), No. 4707 is on an enthusiasts' train for the RCTS, returning from Swindon works, April 1954.

The BR Standard Class '5's were originally used on the Southern and Midland regions although towards the end they did put in an appearance on Western lines as well. This one is No. 73020, dirty, leaking steam and even bereft of front number-plate, although still working hard near Cholsey in December 1965.

With the camera now pointing in the opposite direction we see No. 6823 *Oakley Grange* in charge of the 8.43 a.m. Wolverhampton to Portsmouth service, 13 July 1963. The train is running on the Up main line, and No. 6823 may well be in charge as far as Basingstoke when an engine change will occur.

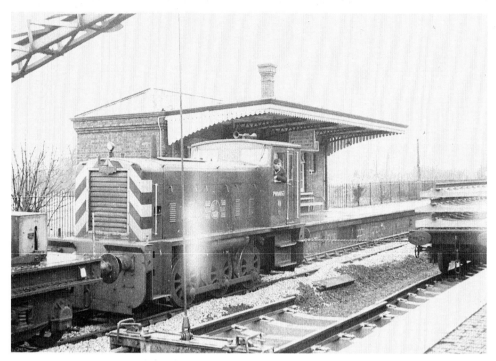

Permanent way work at Cholsey, 12 December 1965. Engineer's diesel No. PWM650 is hauling the relaying crane, and new rails and sleepers are being laid on the Up main line.

Passing the original Cholsey station building, No. 34015 *Exmouth* with another rail tour.

CHAPTER SEVEN

INTERLUDE AT DIDCOT

The steam shed at Didcot still survives as the home of the Great Western Society. Even as late as April 1965 it played host to a number of steam types, including, Nos 2863, 6953, 6993, 6961, 6963, 7923 and one diesel, No. D3959.

On a separate occasion a BR standard Class 4 tender engine, No. 76030 is reversing back on to the shed, seemingly with steam to spare. Again the Western had few of these in the London area, the type seen at Didcot usually working off the DN&S line, although this route finally closed in 1964.

A DMU complete with 'cat's whiskers' at the front. The provision of these yellow lines was to assist those working on the track to see the units approaching, because they were silent compared with steam. Later yellow panels and later still full yellow ends were applied. Known as the first generation of units, these were the ones which initially replaced steam, although few now survive in service. The train is leaving Didcot bound for Oxford.

At Didcot, as elsewhere, an ash shed was provided in the 1940s to mask the glare of hot coals which might otherwise be seen from an enemy aircraft. The buildings themselves were little more than corrugated sheets on a steel framework and suffered badly from corrosion in later years as well as creating even more cramped working conditions. Amid a veritable mountain of ash and clinker No. 6903 *Belmont Hall* is on the disposal lines, February 1965.

Didcot, along with Reading and most other main depots, possessed a lifting shop where various repairs could be carried out. Occupying the facility on 9 May 1965 was No. 3848. On 18 April Oxford Pannier Tank No. 9773 had been resident. The belt-driven machinery was typical and remained in use until the very end of BR operation.

An unusual visitor in the form of 9F No. 92018, once fitted with a Crosti boiler. The engine was recorded alongside Didcot depot, no doubt waiting to return towards its home depot in the Midlands, 15 August 1964.

A green liveried No. 2295 recorded by Wally. It is possible the engine is fresh from a Swindon overhaul and the tender decal suggests it was photographed sometime around 1957/8.

A sad photograph to finish with at Didcot but nevertheless appropriate. No. 7816 *Frilsham Manor* is using the turntable at Didcot for the last time on 13 June 1965, being prepared to take the last two steam engines, Nos 6928 and 7927, dead from Didcot to store at Oxford.

CHAPTER EIGHT

READING & AREA: A FINAL GLIMPSE

The exterior of the magnificent main buildings dating from 1868, complete with the rooftop belvedere. For some time this was one of the high vantage points of the town but has since been dwarfed by modern office blocks. A considerable number of horse-drawn cabs and carriages are visible, dating the view to around the turn of the century. (Lens of Sutton)

The original Brunel design station at Reading, seen from the trackside shortly before rebuilding commenced in 1896. The view was probably taken from the original middle signal-box and shows to advantage the 'one-sided' station in use up to that time. Brunel's ideas for wayside stations had been to have the platforms on one side only, so as to leave the through tracks available for the passage of non-stop trains. Unfortunately the result was congestion and accordingly all were rebuilt in later years in a more conventional form. It is ironic though that less than a century later the station at Swindon was situated on one side of the running lines. (Lens of Sutton)

A special working, undated but probably in about 1910, for the Reading PSA society – what the initials denote is not completely certain. The embellishments on the locomotive are worthy of a second glance as they include the lamps as well. The engine is possibly No. 3351 *One and All*.

More modern times and an unidentified 'Castle' class 4–6–0 rushing through Reading with the London-bound 'Torbay Express' in 1957. (Bob Barnard, collection Hugh Davies)

The interior of Reading West main signal-box in the early years of the century, complete with the signalmen on duty and booking boy. This was the largest mechanical signal-box on the GWR and was originally fitted with a 185-lever frame at the time of opening in 1896, extending further to 222 levers in 1912.

A grey day but a panoramic view of the west end of the station, with the West signal-box visible on the side of the embankment. To the rear is the slaughter house. The lines seen include the Berks and Hants routes curving away to the left and the main line towards Didcot

continuing straight ahead. On the extreme right are the cattle pens and a line of lime-washed cattle wagons. From the number of men visible, complete with spanners and hammers, track maintenance is probably taking place.

Possibly photographed from the top of a convenient signal post, this is the approach to Reading from the Berks and Hants lines, with the main running lines flanked by both carriage sidings and the exit from the steam shed (extreme left). The coaches are

all in the crimson lake livery of the early twentieth century, while in the background is a line of privately owned colliery wagons, including one identified as belonging to Barnsley Main.

One of the small ground frame boxes at the station with various members of staff whose names are unfortunately not recorded. In the background is Vastern Road, which also fronted the signal works.

Changes to the area north of the station and the construction of what may well be an air raid shelter, 1940s. In the background a signal of the plate frame type has been erected experimentally at the signal works. It is to be hoped the engineers had suitably blocked off the siding from use during the work!

Kings Meadow goods depot, which was located just east of the station and at a slightly lower level than the main lines. It was here that transshipment of goods took place with the contents of the various wagons and vans sorted and repacked ready for further movement. The labour-intensive systems, well illustrated in the interior views, also resulted in a greater risk of damage to goods in transit.

An interior shot of Kings Meadow goods depot.

Another view of the inside of Kings Meadow goods depot.

Kennet Bridge signal-box opened in 1899 at a time when traffic was beginning to increase and hence additional break-section signal-boxes were required. This then allowed more traffic to be dealt with. Originally having just eight levers it was soon extended to twenty-one, surviving in use until 1961. (Brian Davis)

West on the main line now and a glimpse of Pangbourne in the early years of the century. As with so many contemporary views of the period the staff are content to be photographed at work. The view includes the relief lines looking towards Reading. (Lens of Sutton)

The next station along at Goring, with the four-track main line which continued as far as Didcot. The very tall signals were a feature of the period and were provided to afford drivers advance warning where a bridge or other obstruction might otherwise impede the view. That on the right is equipped with a wheel at the top of the finial to alleviate the need for the lampman to climb the post when refilling the signal lamp with oil. (Lens of Sutton)

The last of the views on the main line westwards shows Cholsey and Moulsford station which, as the nameboard implies, was the junction for Wallingford. Both buildings date from the latter part of the nineteenth century and yet the Brunel style of chalet design was still being used at this time. (Lens of Sutton)

In connection with the modernization of the Western Region a new diesel maintenance depot was provided at Reading, with facilities which were a far cry from the conditions in the steam shed. The building and its environs are seen here and in the following sequence of photographs, both externally and internally. The front view is somewhat dated by the Ford Anglia parked outside and the types of diesel multiple unit inside are now no longer used in the Reading area.

A train waits in the new diesel maintenance depot at Reading.

An external view of the maintenance depot.

Reading West, or to be more precise Oxford Road Junction. This photograph has been taken to show the reconstructed bridge over Oxford Road. The lines part to serve Didcot, avoiding Reading station, and, to the right, the station itself.

Dean Goods No. 2447 waiting for the road with what is probably a stopping service from Basingstoke, 12 January 1929. This class of engine dated from the 1880s, with the last of the type being withdrawn in the 1950s. Their limited cabs afforded scant protection for the crews. In this particular view the driver appears to be securing something from one of the toolboxes on the tender.

Reading West station freshly painted. Ted Carpenter was stationmaster here for some years. The line is seen curving away towards Southcote Junction and is the point of divergence of the routes to Basingstoke and Westbury.

Auto-train working with a Reading to Basingstoke service on its way south, probably in the late 1920s. A horsebox is also attached to the rear.

Serving the local needs of the town was the GWR's Coley goods yard, which was accessed from the main line by Southcote Junction. Unusually shunting the yard in 1965 in place of the more common pannier tank was 0–6–0 No. 2245 in the last months of its working life. (Hugh Davies)

Bisecting the yard was the main A4 road bridge, and the Kennet and Avon Canal ran alongside. This 1960 view shows timber stacked on open ground, while beyond is the main fan of sidings and coal yard. (Rod Blencowe)

A sight no longer associated with any railway is a yard full of wagons. A variety of commodities are being dealt with here, although it does appear to be primarily mineral and timber based. Today the site has been redeveloped both as a road system and also for industrial and business use. (Rod Blencowe)

Southcote Junction and the divergence of the lines to Westbury and Basingstoke. The necessary diamond crossing here was also equipped with movable toes to facilitate faster running – seen here set for the Westbury route. (Adrian Vaughan Collection)

The interior of Southcote Junction signal-box, probably c. 1955. Despite the railways having been in public ownership for some years by that time, the first aid box still carries the legend GWR, although the interior equipment is a mixture of both old and more modern types.

The small intermediate signal-box at Calcot, which was in place and operating by 1887 purely as a break-section box. It lasted until 1963 although probably, as here, also spent long periods switched out of circuit.

Along the Berks and Hants line to Theale and the timber goods shed as seen in 1965, somewhat decrepit by this time. The siding had originally been to the broad gauge and the entrance certainly indicates its origins by the available width. Much of the site of Theale station has altered beyond recognition after the establishment of the oil and stone terminals, although the station is still open for a lucrative passenger trade. (Philip J. Kelley)

In an effort to combat competition from the increasing number of private carriers the GWR introduced a zonal road lorry system in the 1930s. This is one of the Reading vehicles working at Theale in November 1946.

West to Aldermaston and an example of a 'Challow' type of pressurized paraffin vapour light on its concrete post. This was almost the latest in technology in the 1930s and looks strangely out of place against the background of the Brunel-style station building.

Many of the offices were relocated from Paddington to the shires during the 1940s and Aldermaston became the temporary home to a number of the departments. This then is one of the temporary offices at Aldermaston in 1939, which would serve its purpose, fortunately without interruption, until peace was restored.

A stunning view of one of the former MSWJ 2–4–0s then based at Reading on Aldermaston troughs, with what is probably a Lambourn line working. It was from here that locomotives working the through passenger and goods working were able to replenish their tenders with water, so alleviating the need to call perhaps at Reading in either direction. (Maurice Earley)

An interesting formation for the last view in this compilation running behind Dean Goods No. 2523 near Midgham on a local Berks and Hants line working, *c.* 1925. Today modern looking 'Turbo' units ply the same trade, stopping at the same stations and serving a similar populace. The difference is seventy years and 70 m.p.h. No. 2523 here is unlikely to exceed 30 m.p.h. throughout its trip. Somehow the pace of life seemed more attractive then.